HUZEFA MOTIWALA

Behave Like Humans. ➙ But We are Bears.

Copyright © 2024 by Huzefa Motiwala

All rights reserved. No part of this publication may be reproduced, stored or transmitted in any form or by any means, electronic, mechanical, photocopying, recording, scanning, or otherwise without written permission from the publisher. It is illegal to copy this book, post it to a website, or distribute it by any other means without permission.

This novel is entirely a work of fiction. The names, characters and incidents portrayed in it are the work of the author's imagination. Any resemblance to actual persons, living or dead, events or localities is entirely coincidental.

Huzefa Motiwala asserts the moral right to be identified as the author of this work.

Huzefa Motiwala has no responsibility for the persistence or accuracy of URLs for external or third-party Internet Websites referred to in this publication and does not guarantee that any content on such Websites is, or will remain, accurate or appropriate.

Designations used by companies to distinguish their products are often claimed as trademarks. All brand names and product names used in this book and on its cover are trade names, service marks, trademarks and registered trademarks of their respective owners. The publishers and the book are not associated with any product or vendor mentioned in this book. None of the companies referenced within the book have endorsed the book.

The illustrations in this book are inspired by Cartoon Network's show "We Bare Bears." It has been created using AI and later modified in Photoshop. All rights to the original "We Bare Bears" illustrations are owned by them.

First edition

*This book was professionally typeset on Reedsy.
Find out more at reedsy.com*

Contents

Meet The Characters		iv
1	The Existence	1
2	Whimsy's Date	3
3	Bears in a Supermarket	5
4	Social Media Effect	7
5	Honeycomb's Story Telling Nights	9
6	The Street Encounter	11
7	Whimsy's Cookies	14
8	The Joy Day	17
9	Unusual Zebra Crossing	20
10	The Pizza Trouble	22
11	Entry of Sci.Hannyhani	25
12	The Movie Show	28
13	The Kitchen Mishap	31
14	Electricity Gone	34
15	Unexpected Entry	36
16	The Reveal	40
17	The Call	44
Acknowledgements		47
Author's Note		48
Would Love To Connect		49
About the Author		50

Meet The Characters

1

The Existence

There was one Island faraway in the middle of the sea which was almost abandoned by the other parts of the world. No not because their people were bad or dangerous types or were some breath taking gangsters. Actually the island was trapped by the supernatural things. Like the lady sitting on the broom and flying over the city or animals suddenly start speaking human languages and start living with humans. The residents of the Island were somehow now habitual to this things and was taking everything normally. One day from the forest, one pink color bear with the camera in hand, green color bear and yellow color bear came to the city and stood on the road looking all over here and there. The vehicles got stopped and the road got jammed. Placards was hanging around their necks. Fuzzy, Honeycomb and Whimsy was written respectively. These were their names. The three bears spoke to them in the human language *"Hello Humans."* Although people were surprised by this but were pretty sure that again some sort of supernatural thing has happened. The people of Island accepted the bears peacefully and provided them with everything they needed to live as humans. Besides they have seen so much unusual things so why would they reject the bears which were surprisingly cute and that also in pink, green and yellow color. The life was almost going good between humans and bears and a man who got inspired opened his own cafe on bear theme and Honeycomb, Fuzzy and Whimsy were chief guest.

2

Whimsy's Date

Bear Bistro cafe, a round table, two candles blowing and a sweet romantic music in a background but Whimsy nervously fidgeting with his tie while waiting for his date to arrive. He had carefully chosen a table in the middle that he thought would be more romantic and the light hum of laughter and conversation from the surrounding tables was making the atmosphere more exciting. The date arrived, guiding her to the table, Whimsy extended a paw, expecting her to sit beside him. To his surprise, she sat opposite to him. Whimsy with wide eye open, *"why are you sitting opposite to me? We are not here for the interview. "* *"No, Whimsy, I just thought this spot had the best view of the surroundings."* she commented. Whimsy with an exaggerated pout, *"S-U-R-R-O-U-N-D-I-N-G-S! and what about the romantic tales we could share sitting side by side?"*

In a house, Honeycomb and Fuzzy were enjoying the meal and suddenly the voice came *"Can I join you guys? I have a grilled cottage cheese sandwich with an extra lettuce in it."* Fuzzy couldn't resist the smell and grabbed the bag. *"Whimsy what are you doing here? and what about your date? did she rejected you because you are not fat or you are not that cute as much the soft toy teddy which are sold at the shops?* Honeycomb commented. *"Heyy did you bring that 5 types of dipping sauces that white, red, yellow! cause I am not seeing it in the bag Whi-msy"* Fuzzy asked. Waving with a sad face, pulled out a chair, took a seat and Whimsy said, *"She chose to sit opposite of me and enjoy the surroundings instead of sitting next to me."* and a Honeycomb had a confused laugh. "W-H-I-M-S-Y!!!! you just forgot the lovely dipping sauces" Fuzzy shouted with a brown parcel bag covering his face.

3

Bears in a Supermarket

"*Hey! Fuz-zy, I've just researched about that long sticks the humans keeps rubbing on their teeth in morning and some even at night too. It's one type of ritual to remove the vegetables, fish and yes many other things from the teeth which are just stuck there.*" Honeycomb commented. Fuzzy raises an eyebrow up with a a quizzical expression on his face, "*so they humans after removing the stuck foods from teeth, they eat them again or T-H-E-Y just flow them into B-A-S-I-N-S?*" remarked, his eyes widening in astonishment. A human standing nearby said "*obviously it needs to be flowed I mean washed away as they are dirty you bear with a cap on a head and yes they are called toothbrush.*" "*Ah! okay, honeycomb buy this sticks so called toothbrush as I want to flow some yesterday's lettuce from my teeth!*" Fuzzy commented. A near by human again "*Only toothbrush will not work teddy you also need a toothpaste for that which is right there in that section.*" "*Honeycomb have you researched this paste?*" Fuzzy asked. "*Ya I've, it's somewhat like a jam which we apply on bread. This just need to be apply on sticks ah! I mean toothbrush.*" "*Alright! I'll be picking up the honey flavored one*" Fuzzy grins widely. "*Hey I just asked *one girl for a date!"* voice came from back and it was a Whimsy. Fuzzy in between *"Oh! nice again bear bistro cafe! please don't forget to bring the dipping sauces this time and yes tell them to pack the yesterday's one.."* - *"When you are going is it tonight Whimsy?"* Honeycomb asked interrupting the Fuzzy. *"I don't know, she just hand over this packet of date to me which are 25% off."* his face scrunched up in a puzzled way. *"No worries Whimsy and do you want to pick a toothbrush and a toothpaste to remove the stuck things from your teeth?"* Honeycomb commented. *"Now what is this stuck things mean? see I have a beautiful teeth."* Whimsy posing with a big smile. Honeycomb forming his face in a detective look *"I got you, I've come to know why you are not getting your date."* pausing for 3 seconds - *"You have a Y-E-L-L-O-W teeth and this humans love W-H-I-T-E teeth!"* Fuzzy over excitedly started checking everyone's teeth - *"Hey Mr. can I see your teeth please! - Hello! do you like your teeth to be white like a mozzarella cheese - Hey where are you running? I am not here to afraid you, why are you calling me a whimsical creature."* and suddenly a security person came running towards them. *"Fuzzy! Whimsy! run towards the exit fast!"* Honeycomb shouted. After reaching 500 meters away from the shop *"Hey there was one lady who had no teeth at all."* Fuzzy with a surprised face. From that day - the board got hanged on the door [No Bears Allowed].

4

Social Media Effect

Beep - Beep - screens flashing - mobiles bouncing - tones buzzing. *"F-u-z—zy and Whimsy just cover yourselves this humans would have started a some sort of war."* Fuzzy and Whimsy got hide in the kitchen with the egg pans in a hand and in a stance of dodging bullets. Honeycomb with a brave heart - steadily walking towards the mobile with a black glasses, picks up the phone and boom what he sees - The video in which himself, Fuzzy and Whimsy are being recorded doing that things in the super market earlier. Honeycomb with a happy face *"Hey pals, it's us."* - *"But when did we start the war with this humans.."* Whimsy with a exclamatory mark. *"That's the wrong question, why we have started the war with this humans?? they have invented so so good dishes such like a grilled chicken leg and that sweet kung pao potatoes made up with sauces."* Fuzzy with a sad and irritating face. Honeycomb commented *"No one has started the war! just see this video."* Fuzzy and whimsy watched the video and were getting happy. There were millions of views, likes and comments going on. But suddenly the scene changed from the garden of flowers into a dessert, as in the comments section people were not saying nice things. They were saying mean things for them. Also humans were editing their videos in a different ways. Some people were wearing bear costumes and acting like them. The 3 bears broke. Also the news was coming with a big headlines **"Sales increases for the dolls by 45%, teddy bears falls down by 60%."** And the most unusual line was **"Even the males are seen buying dolls instead of teddy bears."** Whimsy said *"If people are watching, let's show them we can do good things too!"*

5

Honeycomb's Story Telling Nights

After the social media things, bears have arranged the Bear Story Telling Nights in a lovable Bear Bistro cafe. Lights, chairs, tables plus the warm atmosphere was set.
Public who still loved teddy's were occupying a seats. Ahh! also the ones who were not. They were here to get the new fresh content for them to spark the social media. By the smell of pizzas, Fuzzy was not able to sit at a one place. As the waiter walks to a customer Fuzzy was also waving to that path like a flying balloon. A stage was set, a seat was arranged and a mic with a tied bow. Honeycomb with a positive walk sat on a chair, started his talks. *"Welcome to the Bear Story Telling Nights people. I am wondered about these small rectangles with each alphabet written on it. Humans call it a 'keyboard' - coughing - I mean you all sitting here call it keyboard."* Paused for 2 seconds - *"I have researched and observed a bit like a person when face to face doesn't talk anything but through this you can speak for hours. How do you manage with such tiny keys? and what about the emotions that can be felt more clearly only when you are sitting in-person?"* Honeycomb asked with his wide eyes opened and a curiosity

reflecting on his face. One person raised his hand - Honeycomb towards kitchen *"Staff, that person needs something pizza or sandwich please assist him. Sorry sir they are coming."* Again Honeycomb with a serious look *"Fuzzy please can't you take care about other's people eating rather than your eating."* completing his words with a smile. *"No no I don't want to eat anything now, just only I ate a delicious sweet corn bowl prepared with the spices and chutneys. I just want to answer your question which you just asked."* the man replied. *"Oh okay! yes please."* Honeycomb with a smile. But suddenly there was a chaos among a people and don't think wrong it was not for the bears it was about the sweet corn bowl. All were panic to give the orders first but all thanks to Fuzzy as he handled all the chaos quickly plus the Bear Bistro Cafe Staff also took the orders perfectly. When all settled, that person *"We have been provided with emojis to express the emotions. Little faces that show how we're feeling!"* Honeycomb with a agreeing face *"Yes it's really true, I also love finding relevant emojis while chatting with my buddies but I personally enjoy seeing smiles on faces more. Some don't feel like laughing then also they send laughing emojis just for the sake like this Whimsy does. Whimsy never laughs on my jokes when we are sitting together and additionally he makes the faces like somewhat you humans make while eating bitter guard Haha. Similar videos were made on us and everyone started sharing them without knowing the real story. It was all an act of innocence and misunderstanding that turned into a terrible thing. By the way Whimsy is not here he is into doing something good things somewhere."* Honeycomb stood up from the chair *"Okay guys so today's show is over. Always prefer in-person meetings whenever possible and also try to look out what's real and what's not. Bye."* - (Grrr Grrr) Mobile beeps *"Fuzzy now stop sending me these food emojis!"* Honeycomb in a tired face.

6

The Street Encounter

Honeycomb and Fuzzy wrapped up the night, started the journey towards home. They were very happy with the good behavior of people towards them. Instead of walking they were jumping and dancing in the streets with big laughs on their faces and a happy conversations. In between the road, there was one drink can which came in front of the Honeycomb and guess what? in the drunk of happiness, Honeycomb intentionally took his right foot back and hit the drink can hard, which made it fly into the air like a rocket, but this one had a crash landing on a man reading a newspaper, resulting in torn from the center. Honeycomb got afraid and run to the car to hide pulling Fuzzy too. *"Why are we hiding but that will make more more doubt that we have done this. Instead we have to walk with full confidence, follow me."* Fuzzy told Honeycomb with a 110% confidence.
"Okay but why this guy reading out newspaper at night? most of the humans have tradition to read that in morning..!" Honeycomb in a thinking expression. *"Who did it? Who did it? come to me if you have guts C-O-M-E!"* the guy in a angry mode. Fuzzy and Honeycomb walking towards him. *"OH OKAYYYY so it is you bears!*

see see listen we have made dustbins for this okay. You don't have to fly it in a air like this targeting the newspapers." The guy advising them controlling the anger with a deep breath. Fuzzy - *"Yes Yes actually we were targeting the dustbin only."* - *"But here the dustbin does not exist only, do you see any here?"* The guy asked with one eyebrow raised. *"That's the point. Now you get it why does it hit your newspaper? because dustbin is not kept here."* Fuzzy started laughing and the guy too laughed. Honeycomb had a confused laugh. *"You are right, I will be putting the request first thing in the morning for keeping the dustbin. Thank you Bears. Next time you will be having a dustbin here to target."* Guy waving a hand. It was not a end here as honeycomb was having a curiosity and just asked *"Actually I was wondering why you are reading newspaper at night when newspaper is mostly meant for reading in the morning."* The guy answered *"Actually in the morning I like listening songs more. Putting earbuds while traveling to work."*
"Oh okay the modern tradition followed by humans now a days.." Honeycomb commented. *"What tradition? I didn't get that."* The guy asked with a confused face. *"Nothing nothing it's just a casual way of understanding for us bears, good bye have a happy time."* Saying this Fuzzy pulled Honeycomb and walked away with a waving hand. Walking for a little there was a ding dong - bells ringing. It was an ice cream cart. *"Yes what a luck, let's buy some ice cream for our successful night."* Fuzzy stopped the cart excitedly. *"Wow I am so lucky even bears are here to buy my ice creams."* The ice cream man said. *"Yes yes we will, do you have a honey candy?"* Fuzzy asked. *"Honey candy? actually I don't have an idea about a honey candy but I can give you these strawberry, chocolate, butter scotch..."* Ice cream man commented. Fuzzy - *"Okay okay give one black current cup, Honeycomb you?"*
"I'll take a dark chocolate chips and I think butter scotch is perfect

for Whimsy." Honeycomb replied. Ice cream man with a good gesture *"Perfect! let me parcel it for you. I am keeping some ice in the parcel bag so it does not melt off."* *"Thank you! here's your money."* Fuzzy with a smile. *"I have one request, please can we take a photo together? I'll print it and stick on my cart with the slogan 'Even the Bear's buy it! Being an human what are you waiting for?' it will surely help me with the sales."* The ice cream man asked with his teeth wide open, eager to hear yes. Honeycomb with a positive answer *"Yes we are happy to do that, we love taking photos like humans love cheese on every dishes now a days. By the way do you have any candy that has a cheese toppings?"* Ice cream man with an awkward face *"No no ice creams don't have cheese."* *"Thank God!"* Honeycomb with a relief. *"So can we click a photo."* Ice cream man excitedly. *"Yes but actually we are incomplete as our third partner Whimsy is not here with us. He is at home. Without him the photo will be incomplete."* Honeycomb commented and expressed his feelings. *"No worries guys I have a brilliant idea by which the photo will be complete."* Fuzzy said. Fuzzy calls Whimsy. Ring - Ring - Ring - Whimsy picks up the video call. *"Hey Whimsy we were buying ice creams and this man wants to click the photo with us, are you available to give a pose?"* Fuzzy with a big smile. Whimsy - *"Yes yes I am very happy today, bring lot's of ice cream today. Come quickly."* - And Honeycomb, Fuzzy, Ice cream man and a Whimsy posing on a call got clicked.

7

Whimsy's Cookies

Ding - Dong - *"We are here Whim-s-y, open the door!"* Honeycomb standing with a bag of ice cream. Whimsy ran to the door, opened the door, and in the blink of an eye pulled Honeycomb and Fuzzy inside. *"One minute!"* Whimsy said putting his hands on waist. *"What?"* Honeycomb replied. *"Can you sense anything strange with your paws?"* Whimsy asked. Honeycomb seeing his both paws *"What? everything is fine with my paws. I used the human made device nail cutter this two days ago and polished the nails."* *"I am talking about the ice cream Honey-combbb."* Whimsy with a calm voice. *"Oh my honey! exactly where are the ice creams?"* Honeycomb checking his body all over. *"I know where it is."* Fuzzy commented. *"Oh! thanks Fuzzy for keeping them in fridge."* Whimsy with a relief. *"No actually it's outside the main door...it happened like when you pulled us inside that time the bag slipped out and just we entered the room leaving the ice cream behind."* Fuzzy said with a nervous smile on a face. *"F-U-U—Z-Y-Y-Y."* a loud voice came from Honeycomb and Whimsy. A few moments later after enjoying the ice creams, Whimsy revealed what he was doing the whole day. Whimsy opens the oven, the smell of freshly baked cookies fills the air. Removing the tray of cookies *"So guys here are special Whimsy cookies made with unbelievable ingredients you can ever think."* Whimsy said. *"The smell is very nice Whimsy."* Honeycomb with a tongue out. Whimsy hands a cookie to Honeycomb, he inspects the circle cookie from all angles. *"As I have two hands, I'll pick two cookies."* Fuzzy picking up with the yummy expression. As the cookie was moving towards the mouth of Honeycomb and Fuzzy a sudden voice came *"Wait! will you eat this cookies without clothes?"* Whimsy said and smiled. *"Please Whimsy We're not humans we're bears and we haven't started dressing like humans yet."* Fuzzy commented with eagerness to eat. *"No, no, I am not talking about our dress, it's about cookie's dress."* Whimsy said. *"Please don't play with our emotions now, first you hand us cookie and now you are saying that this cookies are unclothed."* Honeycomb with a irritated face. *"haha okay okay keep the cookie here and see what I do."* Whimsy pulls a jar of creamy goodness, it's a vanilla cream. He puts a good amount of cream on the cookies which makes the cookies look beautiful. Fuzzy was just like a person who waits impatiently for the bus so that he does not have to reach office late. But it was not yet finished, after making the delicious layer of cream it was now the turn of the topping. Whimsy peeled the banana, cut it into slices, delicately placed it on top of each cookie. The look of the cookie with a creamy white layer and a slice of banana was like seeing a beautiful view from the top of a mountain. Finally Honeycomb and Fuzzy picked up the cookie, took a bite, the teeth touched the banana slice, got into half, the creamy layer touched the lips and the cookie broke. *"I've never tasted anything like this before. It's very tasty."* Honeycomb mumbled. *"My teeth and tongue fell in love with each other eating this."* Fuzzy said munching. *"So *then lets make this humans go mad with this cookies."* Whimsy with a smile.

8

The Joy Day

So now it was a day when the cookies were to be distributed. All 3 got ready, basket was filled with biscuits. The sun was getting powerful I mean the summer days were getting hotter. All three were wearing caps on their heads and it was a full summer vacation mood. In a cinematic way, Honeycomb stepped out of the door with a black goggle on his eyes. Then Fuzzy stepped out of the door with a basket of cookies and a flying ribbons on the cap. No no as it is a summer so flying of ribbons was not because of wind, it was because of the Whimsy who switched on the mini hand fan for the cinematic stepped out of the door. While humans are fond of cinematic entries, it was then sure that a new trend of cinematic exits had to be started by blowing human minds with this. Finally Whimsy stepped out of the door and closed the door. *"Let's go to the garden, there will be many kids playing around."* Fuzzy commented. *"But in that place we will have to face competition from humans."* Whimsy replied. *"What type of competition?"* Honeycomb asked. *"There will be too many humans who will be targeting the mothers and fathers to sell cotton candy, ice creams, and that popcorn who keeps jumping up down and then they catch them and fill up in those boxes for the kids."* Whimsy explained. *"They will be all charging the money bro, we are distributing just for joy. So it's unlikely we will face any competition."* Honeycomb said. *"Great then."* Fuzzy commented. Finally they reached the nearby garden and took a entry. Honeycomb placed a mat and kept a basket. Now they were looking for a ways to call the kids but what they saw is the huge crowd surrounding the cotton candy seller, some kids were crying as their parents were not interested to catch the jumping popcorns. *"First let's catch the kids who are playing around. Let me try."* Fuzzy commented. Fuzzy saw a child sitting near the slide with a sad face. He approached her. *"Hey kid why are you looking sad?"* Fuzzy asked. *"I can't talk to you."* Kid replied. *"Oh! but why...am I not cute?"* Fuzzy asked making a emotional look, eyes wide. *"I am being told not to talk to strangers."* kid with a face down. *"Oh welllll.....but may be the bad strangers I think."* Fuzzy said. *"If you are a good person, will you play with me?"* kid asked. *"Yes sure."* Fuzzy with a smile. Now it was not that easy for Fuzzy. Fuzzy was to climb up the thin stairs of the slide with his legs and paws. Seeing this, Honeycomb and Whimsy were cheering from there. Fuzzy carefully climbed up murmuring *"I don't know how this small humans I mean kids enjoy this. This is so risky."* Finally Fuzzy reached the heights. *"Come on Fuzzy! you can do it."* Honeycomb in a excited tone. The kid was also very happy and was clapping for Fuzzy. Fuzzy became emotional after seeing the kid and closed his eyes and slid down. As Fuzzy was not aware about this human thing, he did not tried to stop himself and just got crashed on the grass upside down. All the surrounded kids were laughing and getting happy with this act. One kid surrounded by telling his father *"Papa, I don't want a clown in my birthday party, I want this teddy please."* Getting a chance, Honeycomb and Whimsy came to them with a basket of cookies. *"Hello! Kids, do you-u-u like cookies?"* Whimsy asked making a mouth watering look. *"Ye-s-s-sss" kids replied.* Honeycomb and Whimsy started distributing cookies to kids and their parents. All were making a delicious faces and was wondering about these uniquely made cookies. Fuzzy was sitting on the ground and trying to remove the mud and grass from his body and that kid came. She broke the cookie into half and gave the half part to Fuzzy telling *"Thank you for being an extra cheese in my pizza."* Haha. She just told that thank you for making my day wonderful.

9

Unusual Zebra Crossing

Since it was almost noon and Fuzzy's stomach was making noises, they planned a pizza feast. There was a pizza cafe just on the opposite side of a garden. The three bears were standing in the line to cross the road but it was not to be the regular crossing experience as this was the busiest road. As the traffic signal zebra crossing was also a few miles away, this was going to be the most difficult experience for them. Peep-Peep-Peep were the voices coming from all around just like a thunderstorm makes in a sky. Honeycomb takes out the binoculars from bag and zooms in on the traffic signal. *"Guys, I am able to see, green bulb is on."* Honeycomb comments with a serious look. *"Ya, that's the only reason these vehicles are moving. Let us know when it changes!"* Whimsy said. After 5 seconds, *"Ahh! be safe you all, it's yellow bulb now. Don't make a move. Humans tends to move their vehicles at a higher speed on a yellow bulb."* Fuzzy and Whimsy took a one step back. After a few seconds the light turned red, the vehicles started slowing down and stopped near the signal. Since Bears were in the middle, the cars were moving out still to reach the signal and stopping one by one behind. Fuzzy showed the confidence and tried to cross the road and suddenly one bike came in between. *"Hey why are you not stopping your vehicle, its red color bulb there."* Fuzzy commented. *"Why should I stop here? I'll reach near the signal and stop there. There is so much space between."* *"Okay guys, lets run to the zebra crossing and cross from there."* Honeycomb commented. *"Till we reach the zebra crossing, the red light will changed to green."* Fuzzy said. Whimsy got an idea, he stopped the two wheeler and requested to drop him near the signal. Honeycomb and Fuzzy also did the same. Now the 3 bears respectively sat on the two wheeler and cheering up to reach the crossing fast. As they reached, they stood up from the two wheeler and crossed the road at the zebra crossing and the next moment light changed. *"Hey did you notice anything when we crossed?"* Fuzzy asked. *"What?"* Whimsy questioned. *"Humans and even we bears used this but I didn't find any zebras crossing with us at this zebra crossing."*

10

The Pizza Trouble

Finally they entered the Pizza cafe, Fuzzy got melted with the aromas of pizzas like air releases from a balloon. The corner table was empty which was having a good view of the road. To release the tiredness of unusual crossing, they took a seat and enjoyed the cool water. *"Let's order some pizzas, dipping sauces, shakes, garlic breads and whatever else they have."* Whimsy rubbing a hand on his stomach. *"Let me and Fuzzy go and order strategically. You stay here. And don't just start eating these chilli flakes and oregano."* Honeycomb and Fuzzy goes to the counter to order. They got amazed by seeing the varieties, offers and meal options. After discussing, they ordered one cheese blast pizza, one paneer, capsicum, onion and sweet corn pizza, 3 garlic breads, 3 sliced tomato, lettuce and cheese tacos, and one broccoli, sweet corn and cheese quesadillas.

Paid the money, took the token and returned to the table. Fuzzy giving detective look *"Hey, what is this green green bro near your mouth?"* *"What??"* Whimsy rubbed his mouth with his hand with a look of surprise and fear. The oregano bottle lid was half open. It was clear what had happened. After the waiting of

15 minutes, the order arrived. Honeycomb got up and took the plate and walked towards the table. Due to the smell Honeycomb was unable to concentrate on walk and was behaving like some humans who do sleepwalking. Whimsy saw and ran towards the Honeycomb, grabbed the plate *"What are you doing, why are you giving our food to this lady. She is already having her own burgers."* *"Oh, I'm sorry, actually these things smell so good that I got lost in it and started sleepwalking."* Finally it was a round table, 3 bears on a chairs and a plate full of food on it. Fuzzy moved his hand towards the pizza like the bowler bowling at a speed of 150+ km/h. *"Stop! There's something fishy here."* Fuzzy said. *"Wow, you ordered fish pizzas. I 'fish' you bro, I mean I 'love' you bro."* Whimsy said more excitely. *"But we have not ordered fish pizzas!"* Honeycomb added. *"Yes we have not ordered fish pizzas, I am talking about the size."* Fuzzy pointing towards the pizza. *"I don't love you bro."* Whimsy with a sad look. Fuzzy explaining *"When we were ordering, the ones getting delivered to others looked bigger compared to our pizzas."* *"Oh my god! that's not believable and if it is then it's not acceptable."* Honeycomb with a serious look. Whimsy removing the measure tape from the bag *"Take this, humans use this to measure the size. It will help us to examine."* *"Wow! but why are you roaming with this buddy?"* Honeycomb asked. *"I was using this to measure the cookie size while baking so that each cookie gets the same approx size."* Whimsy said. *"Great, handover to me so I can check our pizza."* Fuzzy asked for the measure tape. He measured the size of the pizza and it came 6 inch. He saw around, one guy was picking up the pizza from the counter. Fuzzy approached him and asked *"Hey, can I have your 25 seconds?"* The guy in a confused look *"25 seconds?"* *"Yes you humans with each other typically ask like can I have your two minutes or can I have your one minute so like that I*

want 25 seconds." Fuzzy in a explanatory way. *"Ya sure, why not but can I give you 25 seconds after reaching to the table."* Guy asked. *"Sure"* Fuzzy said. After reaching the table, Fuzzy moved hands towards the pizza and Guy speaks up *"Hey why are you taking my pizza, I have just allowed you to take 25 seconds and not the pizza." "Yes, I understand, I don't want your pizza. Actually I would like to measure the size of your pizza because it looks like the staff gave us a small pizza."* Fuzzy gets a permission to measure and he gets 8 inch. *"Gotcha! our pizza is 6 inch and yours 8 inch. We are cheated. Honeycomb and Whimsy come to the counter asap."* The 3 bears and the Guy and the pizzas were at the counter. *"Why did you do this to us. You have done cheating with us by cutting the size of pizza."* Honeycomb asked. One from staff *"I am sorry it's not fault of our restaurant. It's me who has done this. I just thought that you are bears and you will not get an idea so I just cut out sharply and ate it."* Restaurant manager from behind *"You are fired." "God my pizza has become cold pizza. Please give me a new hot pizza."* Guy with a irritated face. [Laughing voice in the background].

11

Entry of Sci.Hannyhani

[Entry of new character]
Bears have become enough famous in this island. After such tight security of the island, the news of the bears living in the human world reached the Psychology Scientist Hannyhani. She loved learning human behavior. After listening the news she was shocked. She was provided with the photos and videos by which she can believe. The photo of Honeycomb story telling night, video of supermarket chaos, a photo with an ice cream man. *"This is S-O-M-E-T-H-I-N-G out of syllabus thing. I need to visit the neighbor island to see what's happening there. I am pretty sure they are humans wearing a bear costume working in a circus. Let's go and have a cup of tea. Ahh! I mean cup of honey." Sci.Hannyhani with a mischievous smile.* In the night, she took a boat and reached to the island silently. She books a room for her to stay. Prepares the bed and goes to sleep for a exciting morning. The next day - She wakes up, has a breakfast and prepares a plan to reveal the real identity of bears. She asks a near by food stall owner where the bears are staying. He showed her the way. Hannyhani takes a bike on rent and first visited the theatre and

bought 4 tickets. *"Today audience will be enjoying two movies, one with the tickets and one without."* She murmured. Finally she reached the bears house which was now known as The Paws Room. She was scanning the area fully so that she would not be caught doing uncommon things. She wears the white bed sheet over her head and a black sunglasses behaving like a ghost. Goes to the door, places 3 tickets on the door mat and rings the bell and runs a few meters away from the door. Honeycomb arrives at the door, opens, and sees no one. He checks left and right and says to himself *"I think someone is trying to play hide and seek with me."* He closes the door. Hannyhani to herself with the positive vibe *"Yess, I knew it. They are humans. Because most of people don't tend to use brain with an extra effort. Our brain does what we are instructed to do. When bell rings, we need to find the person standing. If not then simply close the door finished. This proves they are humans and not bears."* And suddenly the door opens again, Honeycomb quickly looking here and there to catch the person but is not able to. Suddenly Hannyhani with a different voice *"Hey, please take a look at your mat, you will find something!!"* Honeycomb moves around *"Oh! okay let me. Wow what is this papers? let me check."* Honeycomb closes the door and calls Fuzzy and Whimsy. *"Wow our first letter from a postman."* Fuzzy said. Honeycomb *"No, there was no postman. It was on our door mat. But yes someone was present who guided me to see at a door mat."* *"G-U-I-D-E-D?"* Whimsy asked. *"Yes actually my big fat tummy was blocking me to to see the letters below. Let me see what it is."* Honeycomb with letters in a paw. After seeing the letters, he comes to know that it is a movie tickets. *"Guys these are movie tickets. It's a 8:00 pm show. Hurrayy!"* Honeycomb feels happy and starts dancing. Whimsy joins Honeycomb and dances the tango with him. Fuzzy was little bit surprised by the unknown movie tickets.

12

The Movie Show

So, lights off, movie starts, mobile out. As the intro starts there was a dozens of flashlights flashing in the entire hall. All were recording the intro scenes like the movie title and the entry of the hero. Hannyhani sitting next to Honeycomb *"Don't you want to click videos or pictures. I am sure you would be having a lot's of followers on your social media."* *"Hey! Yes, we have. Next to me is Fuzzy and next to him is Whimsy and he is our social media care taker. But I think the urge to do this does not fall under our genes actually."* Honeycomb said. *"Oh yes I see."* Hannyhani with a smile. As the movie progresses, there is a pink drop silence among all and the cool temperature of the AC starts. After about half an hour of the movie suddenly a voice came from the corner. It was sound of the person's snoring. *"The story of the movie is going so great and this person is sleeping here."* Fuzzy said. The person next to the sleeping guy wakes him up and says *"Hey man take my card, my clinic address is mentioned on it. Meet me between 3:00pm to 5:00pm."* The sleeping guy in a sleepy way *"But why?"* *"It's because that next time you'll less snore or will not snore so others can see the movie well and you can sleep well."* Next to guy delivered the master pitch. *"In this era anything is possible, to enjoy the air condition and sleep well all are choosing movie theaters."* Hannyhani to honeycomb. *"Yes, I think so. As far as I have researched humans brains are evolving very rapidly."* Honeycomb replied. *"Yes. Even you are human. Just wearing the bear clothes and making people enjoy like a live circus."* Hannyhani speaking in a low voice into Honeycomb's ear. *"No no we are not circus people. I am a pure bear. We are a pure bears origin. I think you are new here."* Honeycomb said. *"Yes I am a tourist here."* Hannyhani replied. *"Hey let's open up popcorns. The story is giving goosebumps and due to that my stomach needs some food."* said Fuzzy rubbing his stomach. *"Checkmate, the story is giving rising tensions and due to that the hormones are released and cause humans feel to eat. You are H-U-M-A-N-S not B-E-A-R-S."* Hannyhani excitedly notes it down in her writing pad. *"Do humans eat 20KG to 40KG food daily before sleeping for continuous 2 months to 6 months?"* Whimsy asked. *"Nooo. We humans don't eat that much and also not sleep this much. This is not our things, I think you are referring the Bears thing."* Hannyhani replied. *"Yes. This is our thing and we were doing it. So this proves that we are Bears."* Whimsy with a smile. *"Sshh.. keep silence."* Someone from an audience. It was not easy for Hannyhani as it was not an usual psychologist interaction between humans. It was an uncommon interaction with Bears. As the movie was progressing and becoming intense there came the voice of crying. It was a baby. Fuzzy disturbingly *"Who is crying? I think someone has become very emotional."* *"She's just a baby."* Hannyhani said. *"oh! but my honey why this person is making very silly faces. Why he is making baby crying for no reasons."* Fuzzy with a surprised face. *"He is making strange faces so that the baby stops crying. Baby enjoys this type of faces and starts laughing."* Honeycomb explained. *"It's so strange being human, some is coming for sleeping and some are bringing their babys here so that they can make strange faces."* Fuzzy with a clueless face. Here it was not over. It was more things to come. C-R-U-N-C-H # C-R-U-N-C-H # S-L-U-R-P sound came from behind. Someone was enjoying the snacks more than a movie. Suddenly the drink can got pressed and the contents spilled out on the Whimsy. "Wow, this theater is giving real experience. It looks like I am really wet." Whimsy suggested. *"Theatre is not giving real like experience, you are experiencing a wet because you are really wet."* Hannyhani said. The person from behind *"Sorry Bears I am really sorry. Actually the friend next to me gave the pinch and it all happened."* *"Why your friend is pinching you but?"* Fuzzy asked. *"Actually I was going to speak up the climax which she did not wanted to listen. If you want to then I can tell you actually the end will be like...."* As soon as he was about to tell the climax one other person just thrown the sauce on his face.

13

The Kitchen Mishap

After the theatre mishaps and a good conversation with Hannyhani, they 3 decided to do a good get together with Hannyhani at their house. It was a dinner and a gossip plan. When Hannyhani got invited she became happy that she got a chance to know more about that as due to theatre mishaps she was not able to reveal much. Honeycomb, Fuzzy and Whimsy gone to supermarket and bought the vegetables and meat. They were excited as they had never done the home dinner party like this before with any humans. Reaching home first they slept for few hours. Upon waking they start cooking.

"Whimsy cookies are less, let me bake more" Whimsy said. *"Yes, and you have to make a roasted fish too. We just love it."* Fuzzy said. *"I am preparing ladyfinger gravy, cottage cheese dip in spinach gravy, and butter chicken. It will be perfect! what you think?"* Honeycomb asked. *"Yes bro. And let me takeover the tortillas."* Whimsy said. *"I'll cut all the vegetables and prepare the ingredients till that."* Fuzzy suggested. All three wore aprons and started on their mission. Whimsy took the oven area and the rest Honeycomb took. Fuzzy took the hall area and laid the mat with the all

the ingredients. He started cutting the ladyfinger into small pieces. *"We have bought East Asian ladyfingers, it has worms in it. And they love eating worms but our guest is an American."* Fuzzy commented. Honeycomb educating *"it's not something like East Asian ladyfingers. That's the damage piece. Throw it away."* By hearing this Fuzzy throws the lady finger in the air and gets splash on the Whimsy face. Whimsy starts dancing and jumping here and there. *"Whimsy is very excited for the feast. See his unique dance steps."* Fuzzy with a cheering claps. *"This is not my steps. Worms are forcing me to. Please do something."* And Whimsy bumps into Honeycomb. Honeycomb had put the mixer grinder which jumps up and the spinach gravy spills out in the entire kitchen. Fuzzy turns on the vacuum cleaner and sucks up the worms. *"Our home has become totally messed now. It's all because of you Fuzzy."* Honeycomb with a irritated face. *"I am really sorry but it's not fully me. Whimsy is also a crime partner in this."* Fuzzy commented. *"Now please stop playing the blame game like humans. This is how they play by putting it on others. Now you please go to the near by store and bring the spinach. Other things we will manage."* Honeycomb commented. *"Okay...."* Fuzzy said with a low and sad voice. Whimsy and Fuzzy started focusing on preparing food first and then decided to clean the mess off. Fuzzy reached the supermarket, goes towards the leafy vegetables section. Fuzzy's mind gets out of control by seeing all the leafs and gets highly confused. He asks the lady near by. *"Excuse me ma'am, please help me identify spinach."* Fuzzy asked for help. *"Sure, that red bucket has spinach in it."* lady respond. *"Oh, Thank you very much. Happy shopping."* Fuzzy greeted. *"Last time it was a total chaos created by us in a supermarket but now things are under control. I am managing well, just bill the spinach at the counter and the job is done."* Fuzzy to himself. On the other hand Whimsy and Honeycomb were near to finish off the cookies, tortillas and the gravy. Just the cottage cheese was left. Fuzzy reached the counter and there were other customers too. everyone had placed their groceries on the table. Fuzzy also kept his spinach on the table. As the guy was busy counting the money, Fuzzy's spinach got billed. But it was misfortune. The cashier picked up the fenugreek leaves of the near by guy and packed it up for Fuzzy. Fuzzy was coming home happily. Suddenly the black cat came and crossed the way. *"OH-MY Honey why did you do this to me dear cat. B-U-T everything is fine. Everything is going almost perfect. Visited supermarket, bought spinach, billed, will handover to Honeycomb. Perfect. It is just a human superstition that they are believing."* Fuzzy to himself. *"Meow" cat responded.*

14

Electricity Gone

Fuzzy reached home, rings the bell. Whimsy comes at the door, opens it. Fuzzy handed the bag. *"Wow, the smells are so good. Where is Honeycomb?"* Fuzzy asked. *"He became very tired. So he has gone to take a hot bath. I need to prepare a spinach gravy now."* Whimsy replied. Whimsy takes out the leaves from the bag. *"Wait a minute, Why this is looking like a fenugreek leaves, wait a minute you have bought fenugreek leaves. F-U-Z-Z-YYYYYYY."* Whimsy with a high tone and a red face. Fuzzy confused and in a sad way *"It's not my fault. It's all because of black cat."* *"Let me take out some curd and make fenugreek leaves gravy."* Whimsy winked. *"Yes, you saved me! and I'll clean the house."* Fuzzy suggested. Whimsy started preparing the curry and Fuzzy started cleaning the house. Fuzzy was unaware that there was more to come from him. It was almost 15 minutes passed and all was going well and suddenly Fuzzy decided to use the vacuum cleaner. He turned on the vacuum cleaner, the geyser in the bathroom was also on. The electricity got clashed. Lightening happened, Lights off. *"W-H-A-T...W-A-S...T-H-A-T..."* Honeycomb yelled from inside the bathroom. *"Oh my honey what just this happened."* Fuzzy in fear. *"I don't know what this Fuzzy is upto today. First damaged ladyfinger, then fenugreek spinach replacement and now this."* Whimsy said in a troubled way. *"Fenugreek spinach replacement?"* Honeycomb questioning. *"I am doing nothing, this is all happening without my participation."* Fuzzy exhausted. *"Uff! Honeycomb I am giving you a candle. It will give a brightness."* Whimsy said. Whimsy light up the candles all over the room. *"Wow, looks like we got to have a candlelight dinner."* Fuzzy with a satisfying breath. *"It's soooo awesome. I don't have words to describe. The atmosphere is like a softest puff with a little butter, thick layer of creamy goodness in the middle with a juicy sweet strawberry pieces."* Honeycomb in a amazed way when he came out of a bathroom. *"Yeah, wait where is this water coming from on my feet?"* Whimsy asked. *"What ever the honeycomb told was completely mouth watering."* Fuzzy with a mouth open and a saliva falling by.

15

Unexpected Entry

Ding-Dong bell rang, it was Hannyhani at the door. About 2-3 minutes passed but the door was still not open. There was a kind of chaos going on inside. Hannyhani was able to hear at some level. Actually they were fighting that who will open the door and greet her to the house. During the chaos, Honeycomb got an idea. Honeycomb tied a rope to the door handle and they stood a few meters apart. All 3 dragged the rope and the door opened. Hannyhani felt relief that she finally got the entry. She stepped into the house and in front of her they were standing. *"A warm welcome to our house Hannyhani." they greeted.* Hannyhani was amazed by the atmosphere. She moved a little further and the bucket from above overturned and rose petals fell on Hannyhani. *"Wow, so unique welcome experience. Thank you bears." "Our pleasure, please sit."* Hannyhani takes a seat. Whimsy brings a dish of welcome drinks. They all sat and started talking. *"The drink is very nice. The mint flavor is perfect."* Hannyhani praised. *"So you play with human brains right?"* Fuzzy asked. *"Haha I don't play with brains Fuzzy."* Hannyhani replied laughing. *"Yes I knew it. I told Honeycomb firstly that brain is not a toy to play with."* Fuzzy said excitedly. *"It was a slang Fuzzy."* Honeycomb commented. *"Basically I try to understand how people think, feel and act. We help them to see the things in a different way so they can manage their feelings."* Hannyhani in an explanatory way. *"Okay okay got it."* Fuzzy said. *"Let me set up the music."* Whimsy suggested. Whimsy turns on the speaker. The ad came. There was no skip option given. It played for almost 3 minutes. But they were not lucky enough. The second ad played. Now the skip option was available but after the 1 minute. *"This is the thing which humans highly need to solve it out."* Whimsy in a frustrated way. *"But they are created by humans only."* Honeycomb commented. *"I was traveling by bus one day. The person sitting next to me started talking. I asked him that don't you listen to music like others? I mean it was good that he was more interested in talking with others and not in listening to music. He replied that he was irritated with ads. He had to travel a short distance only and ads are so long that before it gets completed his destination arrives."* Fuzzy said, everyone started laughing. Honeycomb took the mobile and installed one app. *"Use this app called 'Zene' it's like a bird without a cage. One fine human who just made his contribution to the world which you humans call it startup. The music network with zero ads."* Honeycomb advised. *"I'm catching the bus first thing tomorrow to give him this as a gift. I definitely think he hasn't noticed."* Fuzzy commented. *"By the way how did you come up with the idea of candlelight dinner?"* Hannyhani asked. Whimsy giving a confused laugh *"It was just naturally. Nothing much complex."* And the bell rang. Honeycomb got up and opened the door. It was a electrician. *"I got a complain of electricity clashed ahh I mean short circuit."* he said. *"I think there is some confusion."* Honeycomb trying to defense. *"Then why is it dark here and candles are burning?"* Electrician said. *"Because we are having a candlelight dinner. Look, there are different types of dishes kept on the kitchen table."* Honeycomb played a master stroke. But the game was not completed. Electrician with a yorker ball *"So the dinner is not yet started. You can turned on one light so I can write here in the paper and cancel the complain."* "Actually but hmmmm yesss we are having candlelight talks actually so how can I turned on. Hope you can understand and come tomorrow." Honeycomb said without realizing what he's saying. *"Okay okay may I know who is Mr. Fuzzy here?"* Electrician asked. Hannyhani interrupts *"Yes here he is. Fuzzy, you filed a complaint?"* "Actually ya I forgot, now I remembered. Our Fridge is not working actually so for that." Fuzzy handled the situation. *"Oh Fuzzy dear, for that electrician is not the right person. You need to call technician."* Hannyhani explained. "Oh okay I see. I thought the electricity is not able to travel to the fridge because of the burned wires so." Fuzzy suggested. Hannyhani got confused. *"Hey wait, where did the electrician go? Who matters? What matters is that in the end he left."* Honeycomb with relief. Honeycomb closed the door and turned back and shocked to see that electrician has reached the fridge and doing something. *"It's short circuit here. Need to repair the electricity box."* Electrician commented. *"You are so committed guy towards your work."* Whimsy making out a face. *"O-K-A-Y-Y now I see how the plan was made naturally and not complex. There is a short circuit here and that is why candles are burning and windows are wide open for air."* Hannyhani with half eyes closed. *"This is all because of this F-U-Z-Z-Y-Y-Y.........."* Whimsy shouted. *"What I can say is come on let's enjoy the food."* Till then electrician completed the work and they also completed the food. Hannyhani was very happy and liked the food very much. She was having tears of joy. Whimsy handed his special cookies packed in a box to the electrician and he leaved with a smile.

16

The Reveal

So, the room got the lights finally and fans started. Hannyhani confessed that *"Actually the movie tickets which were outside on your door mat was kept my me. I thought that you are humans and would be bored by the daily routines so you are trying to live it in a different way. So I traveled here to reveal your identity. But you are looking real bears as your behavior is not like us."* *"So you are not our friend, you are just a S-P-Y who has come here for M-I-S-S-I-O-N."* Honeycomb commented and informed Fuzzy and Whimsy to be cautious. *"No wait, I think she is a good human."* Whimsy commented. *"Yes I am your friend and not an enemy. And I am very much happy by your hospitality. You are very good bears."* Hannyhani expressing gratitude. *"No problem Hannyhani, and I also understand that who would believe these pink, yellow and green color bears are real bears."* Fuzzy said and laughed. *"Yes it's true, as now you are real bears can I know your origin story that how did you come up like this in human world especially changing your colors. This news will shake off the world."* Hannyhani asked with curiosity. *"Not much I think as according to internet articles, our Island is abandoned by the other parts of the world. They think the people of this island are mysterious and unusual."* Honeycomb commented. *"Yes, I have heard about some incidents that happened here. Especially forest stories."* Hannyhani said. *"Yes, that supernatural incidents have caused this island go lonely. We are also the victims of that. The other parts of the world would be assuming that the Island people would have lost their behavior sense and are doing abnormal things. But the good thing happened, as the video of our bear storytelling night went viral, it was able to change the perspective that they had towards the people of our island. But as soon as they come to know that we are not humans who dresses like bears and are real bears, they will come back to their original thinking. I think they will never be able to accept us the way the people of this island have done."* Honeycomb with the accepting tone. *"Don't worry bears, but instead of this, you should be more concerned about your survival. Do you have any clue about yours. You was saying something that you are victims of forest."* Hannyhani asked in a tense face. *"Yes, we found a fallen camera in a forest which has recorded the entire incident. Do you remember a few years ago there was a talks about witch incident?"* Whimsy asked. *"Yes, I remember! The media department was giving the statements like – a woman sitting on a broom flying over the supermarket, with a bag hanging on a broom on her way to pick up some vegetables!"* Hannyhani said laughing. *"Yes and it was real."* Whimsy said. *"Oh my God, but I think the team was researching it but the woman was not seen afterwards and there were no further reports from the media and the case remained unsolved."* Hannyhani commented. *"That woman was very foodie. She took my fish from my hands and flew away."* Fuzzy making a irritated expression. *"Wait! what? how? when did you meet her and why did she took your fish? guys now I am getting scared. Is that witch woman present here?"* Hannyhani looking all over the room shockingly. *"Actually when I was having a raw fish in my paw I was a bear but something happened and I became human alike. As humans eats cooked food, she thought that this raw fish would be of no use to me and she took away."* Fuzzy replied. *"Fuzzy please don't scare him. Don't worry that woman is not here. Keep calm. Let me tell you what actually happened that day. All three of us were animals, meaning bears living in the forest. One day, while walking, we reached the edge of the forest near the city. The sound of a child crying came to our little ears. There we saw a small child sitting under a tree. The baby was crying hard and so we were trying to get closer. I was just trying to say stop crying by shaking my paw. And in that one woman came flying sitting on a broom and stood there. She thought that we are going to cause harm as we are wild animals so she started doing some actions by which we get afraid and get back. And I stood up on two leg waving both my paw expressing that we will not cause any harm but she took it in the opposite way. She got baffled and without thinking she chant the following phrase – 'BEHAVE – LIKE – HUMANS' this chant traveled to our ears and our world changed. Our brains started giving shocks same like a human feels when a lemon juice falls on the tongue. We started behaving like humans. We become Human alike. But it was not yet finished. One girl came running there and asked the woman that she had written almost all the colors, only three colors are missing. It seems like she was asking about her homework. The woman checked the written colors and found the missing colors which had been forgotten by the little girl. The woman stick was still pointed towards us and she said PINK, GREEN, YELLOW. So now you can see that how we've got these colors."* Honeycomb said and took a deep breath. Listening this Hannyhani's eyes got big and and a jaw dropped. She said *"This is extremely overdose for me and also now it's pretty late. I am not able to digest and need to*

take a pills. I guess now I should leave. I see you tomorrow guys."
saying that Hannyhani was leaving and Fuzzy handover the box of Whimsy's special cookies to her.

17

The Call

The cafe Receptionist of a Bear Bistro cafe with a little stomach out was sitting at his desk, taking hiccups and humming a music. It was afternoon 2:o'clock and was just falling into the nap, the phone rang. He in a fast motion picked up the receiver. *"H-HELLO? Bear Bistro Cafe how may I help you?"* trying to get out of a doziness he asked. The voice on the other hand was filled with hardness and a strict tone - *"Listen up, the person who is always with a plate of doughnuts! I've got some important information for you."* Receptionist making a glance look at the plate of doughnuts on his table *"Hey who are you and how can you talk with me this way."* he replied turning face into red. The other side on the call- *"Relax!, ugh! this is the only reason I was not preferring the bears cafe. Bears are so hot-tempered and you employees have also adapted that nature. Haha never mind. Now listen, I've gonna make a big F-O-O-O-D heist in your cafe so be prepared for it."*

Receptionist rubbing his left eye in a confused state trying to understand the thing which he just listened. *"Wait is this a funny prank going on!? A F-O-O-D HEIST in a cafe!!"* Receptionist replied in a shocked reaction. Taking pause for two seconds, he again asked *"What do you want from us and who are you speaking?"* The other side on the call - *"Yes - you hear it right poor fellow and all is I want from you is a full stocked fresh food prepared in your cafe. Have a nice day."* phone hanged on the other side. Without wasting a second, he dialed the manager's extension - The most unique and hardworking cafe Manager you'll ever meet. He manages the entire cafe from the comfort of his bath tub. Yes you read it right, instead of a traditional office chair Manager has build a third floor height swimming pool jumping board to sit and deal with daily activities. Below a white shining water bath tub as whenever he takes break he stands on the swimming pool jumping board and jumps into the bath tub which has hot water to relax. And as it is situated on the edge of the island, the room is surrounded with the large big transparent glasses giving a view of sea. *"Sir."* Receptionist said, when the Manager answered the call. In a one breath Receptionist said *"I just received the anonymous call saying the food heist is going to happen."* Manager on the other side *"Don't worry be calm, police are present in a city doing their excellent jobs. They will prevent the heist from happening. But W-A-I-T a second why did we received a call about a heist?"* *"Because it is going to be in our cafe Sir!* Receptionist said in a low voice. Manager got stern, a jaw dropping *"What?"* came out with a eyes getting bigger in size with a rising tension about to chopped his nails between his vibrating pair of teeth. He called an urgent meeting in his office. All the top level staff gathered in an office from cafe in an hour, especially the kitchen department. *"Hello! everyone my dear family members."* greeted by Manager. Manager further said *"We the Bear Bistro Cafe has received a threatened call..."* and suddenly the big burp sound comes in between and all gets attracted.

BEHAVE LIKE HUMANS. ➡ BUT WE ARE BEARS.

Manager feels disturbed, asks loudly *"who was T-H-AT."* It was from a CCTV surveillance department head. He is always on the lookout for any suspicious activity. But as his job is like sitting on a chair and keep staring the cameras all over a day, he keeps eating whatever delicious treat he can get and making a burps all over everywhere. *"You will be the main watcher, all your big eyes should be roaming all over the areas of a cafe. It will be nice if you can get yourself rid out of a unnecessary meals you keep having all day and give a bit more focus on the activities going on in our cafe."* CCTV surveillance head in a confident voice *"Y-E-S sir don't worry, nothing will be missed from my eyes."* with a franky falling out from a pocket. *"According to the information the food heist is going to take place in our cafe so you Chef, you have to be extra cautious about the surrounding activities happening near the kitchen and a food inventory block."* Manager informed. As Manager addressed the news, murmuring sounds started to begin. He said *"I am asking all of you to be active. Keep your eyes and ears open for any unusual behavior."* The staff nodded in agreement. The manager continued *"if anyone of us encounter a situation that is beyound our control, we will immediately call the police station and they will do the needful."* Manager's eyes scanning all the staff and his hands on the table in a strict position *"Remember , we are responsible for the safety and well-being of our guests. Let's do everything in our power to ensure that they are safe."* With that the meeting was dismissed. Speaking this much Manager got tired, stood on the swimming pool board and jumped into the bath tub. The staff dispersed with the unsolved questions running in their minds. Who was on the other side of the call? Why did he choose the Bear Bistro Cafe. Only he knows.

Acknowledgements

I would like to express my deepest gratitude to all those who have supported me throughout the writing of this book. My heartfelt thanks to my family and friends for their endless encouragement. Karan Shroff, thank you for being such a great friend and for designing the perfect cover for my book. Lastly, to all my readers, thank you for joining me on this journey.

Author's Note

Behave Like Humans ➡ But We are Bears started as a whimsical idea. My love for cartoons and animation movies gave me the motivation to have mine too. The adventures of Fuzzy, Whimsy, and Honeycomb grew into a story about friendship, bonding, humor, and the unexpected challenges that life throws our way. Tried to show daily human activities from a non-human perspective and how things have changed and evolved over the ages. Writing this debut book has been an incredible adventure, and I hope it brings as much joy to you as it did to me.

Would Love To Connect

Will love to connect with you. Reviews and feedback are most appreciated! Did I bring a smile to your face? What was your favorite scene, or what surprised you the most?
Email ➡ huzyzm786@gmail.com
Instagram ➡ authormotiwala

About the Author

Huzefa Motiwala loves traveling and stuffing mouth with yummy food. Watching cartoons and animation movies makes him happy so he started writing his own whimsical humor cartoons. He loves make people laugh and happy!

Made in the USA
Middletown, DE
07 June 2024